2/99

P9-EJZ-373

COLLECTIONS
of SOUTHWESTERN
POTTERY

Candlesticks to Canteens,
Frogs to Figurines

by ALLAN HAYES AND JOHN BLOM

Photographs by JOHN BLOM

NORTHLAND PUBLISHING

To Carol & Brenda,
who are still hanging in.

Also by the Authors
SOUTHWESTERN POTTERY:
ANASAZI TO ZUNI (1996)

Text type set in Minion
Display type set in Phaistos
Edited by Stephanie Bucholz
Production by Trina Stahl
Production supervised by Lisa Brownfield

Manufactured in Hong Kong by Sing Cheong Printing Co. Ltd.

Copyright © 1998 by Allan Hayes and John Blom
All rights reserved

This book may not be reproduced in whole or in part,
by any means (with the exception of short quotes for the
purpose of review), without permission of the publisher.
For information, address Northland Publishing Company, P.O.
Box 1389, Flagstaff AZ 86002-1389.

FIRST IMPRESSION
ISBN 0-87358-721-9

Library of Congress Cataloging-in-Publication Number 98-18368

Hayes, Allan.
    Collection of Southwestern pottery : candlesticks to canteens,
frogs to figurines / by Allan Hayes and John Blom ; photographs
by John Blom. — 1st impression.
        p.   cm.
    Includes bibliographical references and index.
    ISBN 0-87358-721-9
    1. Indian pottery—Collectors and collecting—Southwest, New.
2. Indians of North America—Antiquities—Collectors and
collecting—Southwest, New. I. Blom, John. II. Title.
    E78.S7H38 1998
    738.3'089'97079—dc21   98-18368

0673/10M/6-98

38.3
1AY
998

☀ CONTENTS

Mojave, Elmer Gates, 1980

☀ Pots, Potters, & Places

⏩ Southwestern American Indian Pottery has a way of
burrowing into your affections.

We know. In 1992, we knew almost nothing about it. Now, we've bought
so many pots that our friends have long since tired of kidding us about "the
John & Al Museum." Yes, we bought all those pots because we fell in love with
the history and tradition behind them, but we also bought all those pots
because collecting is fun.

Sure, we started out looking for treasures—important examples of the
potters' art—but we found ourselves captivated at almost every point by little
pieces that ranged from the eccentric to the truly silly. These included odd
replicas of normally functional household items (things like uncleanable
ashtrays, unwashable dishes and fragile, delicate baby rattles), strange little
creatures not found on this or any other planet, and images of questionable
deities probably invented solely to sell to souvenir-hunting tourists.

These little pieces came into our lives much more quickly and much
more easily than the serious stuff. One reason, of course, is that the little
pieces cost less. As we visited shops and galleries across the country, we found
that it was more fun when we had a quest, even more fun when the quest was
for strange and unusual things, and best when those strange and unusual
things didn't cost very much.

But that's not the only reason, and it isn't the main one. We suspect the
real reason we gathered all these pieces is simply that many of them made
us smile.

Ancient traditions and refrigerator magnets. Southwestern Indian
pottery, at least the part of it that isn't obvious mass-produced kitsch, is still
made according to all or most of the same methods of potterymaking that
have been around for two thousand years. Even some of the most bizarre and
inexplicable creations are stubbornly traditional in the way they were made.

Somehow, Southwestern potters manage to make whatever they make
without forgetting where it all began. They stay within age-old design
conventions, and they stay with age-old techniques, grinding their own clay,
making their own pigments, shaping their pieces by hand, and firing them

outdoors. And many potters still go all the way, making tradition-bound pieces like the large one on the left. Now, that's not to say that no potters today ever take a shortcut now and then. Some buy precast pots (called "greenware") and decorate them with store-bought paints, then fire them in the kiln at the craft shop, and you'll see a few of those on the following pages. But you'll see far more, including some of the silliest, made the good old-fashioned way.

Now

Then

Laguna, Myron Sarracino, 1993 (top);
Mogollon, Tularosa Black-on-white, ca. 1050

Inner Beauty vs. Outer Fun. Any serious book on this subject spends a lot of time talking about the surface characteristics and artisitic integrity that make some pots more equal than others. After all, this is an important art form, and when you're discussing an art form, you have to try to define the elements of that elusive ingredient called "quality."

This is not a serious book. Here, those bets are off. Or at least most of them. If you're looking for pieces that make you smile, you can't get all hung up about purity of intent. Instead, you pick a category like "Christmas ornaments" (probably a good one—it's one that we haven't gone after particularly, so there should be quite a few pieces left). Then you look for it. If you see one, you buy it. Every so often, you'll see one you think is so boring or awful you'll pass it up, but if you really get into the spirit of the thing, you'll be amazed at how low your standards can sink.

Playing the game. If you take up the challenge, you might find yourself looking for, say, salt shakers or owl figurines. And if you buy a few, you're in danger of becoming a collector.

But take heart. Unlike many forms of collecting, this particular game is relatively risk-free.

The majority of the pieces in this book aren't rare or hard to come by. They've been rolled out for tourists for the last hundred years, and there are tens— probably hundreds—of thousands of them out there waiting for a good home.

Oddments

Hot air balloon, Clarice Aragon, Acoma, 1993; horno, Serafina Pino, Zia, 1997; cowboy hat, Hopi, ca. 1935

Most of the pieces in this book cost us under $100, and a few cost under $5. We found hundreds within a few miles of our homes, without traveling to Arizona or New Mexico. Once you scratch the surface, you'll uncover these things everywhere—in Indian craft stores, in antique stores, in thrift shops, at shows, at garage sales, in attics. It seems as if almost everyone has a grandmother, an aunt, or an in-law who brought one home from a Southwestern vacation.

Las Vegas NV to Las Vegas NM, Durango CO to Durango MX, sort of. When we say these pieces come from the "Southwest," we're talking about a nice, easy-to-grasp area. But when we talk about the people who made them, we're talking about people from perhaps thirty locations who speak (or spoke) a dozen or more different languages. To help you understand what you're looking at, here's a map.

It shows who the major and minor players are—the bigger the dot, the more pottery that particular pueblo or tribe produces. It helps to know a bit about all this when you run across something in a junk shop.

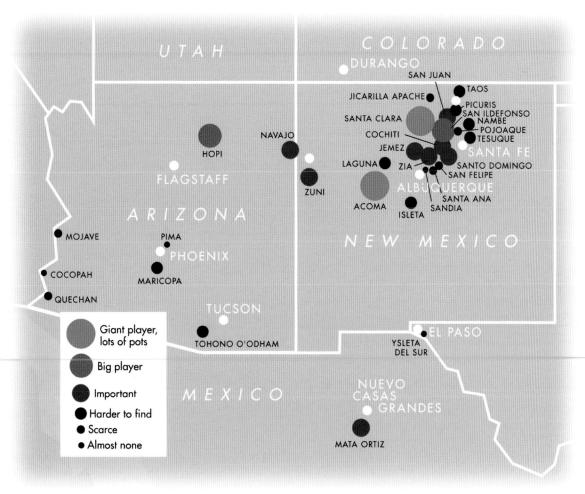

If you don't like reading maps, here's a list of the top thirty, with a pronunciation guide that's close enough to keep people from looking at you strangely when you try to say the words.

Giant Players (lots of pots)
ACOMA (OCK-o-ma). Due west of Albuquerque.
SANTA CLARA. Between Santa Fe and Taos.

Big Players
HOPI (HO-pee). Northeast of Flagstaff.
SAN ILDEFONSO (San Il-de-FON-so). Down
    the road from Santa Clara.

Important
COCHITI (CO-chit-tee). Halfway between Santa
    Fe and Albuquerque.
JEMEZ (HAY-mis). North of Albuquerque.
MATA ORTIZ (MOT-ta Or-TEES) OR CASAS GRANDES.
    Eighty miles south of New Mexico's bootheel.
NAVAJO (NAV-a-hoe). Most of northern Arizona.
SAN JUAN (San WAHN). Halfway between Santa Fe and Taos.
SANTO DOMINGO. Near Cochiti, to the east.
ZIA (ZEE-ya). Just east of Jemez.
ZUNI (ZOO-ny). West New Mexico, almost in Arizona.

Harder to Find
ISLETA (Iz-LET-ta). South of Albuquerque.
LAGUNA. (La-GOO-na). Across the street from Acoma.
MARICOPA. Near Phoenix.
NAMBÉ (NOM-bay). Near Santa Fe.
PICURIS PICK-ur-eese). In the mountains south of Taos.
TAOS (Touse, like "mouse.") Ninety miles north of Santa Fe.
TESUQUE (Te-SOO-ky). Santa Fe suburb.
TOHONO O'ODHAM (To-HO-no Oh-OHD-hum). Down near Tucson.

Mortar and pestle, Sadie Adams, Hopi, ca. 1970; wind chime, Jennifer S. TsePe, San Ildefonso, 1995; buttons, Zia, ca. 1935

Scarce

JICARILLA APACHE (Hick-a-REE-ya). West of Taos.
MOJAVE (Mo-HOVV-ay). On the California border, near Needles.
POJOAQUE (Po-HOCK-ey). Next to Nambe.
QUECHAN (KWAY-chon) OR *YUMAN*. On the California border, near Yuma.
SAN FELIPÉ (San Fe-LEEP-ay). South of Santo Domingo.
SANTA ANA. East of Zia, south of San Felipe.

Almost None

COCOPAH (CO-co-pa). On the California border, around Blythe.
PIMA (PEE-ma). Near Phoenix, on lands shared with Maricopa.
SANDÍA (San-DEE-ya). A tiny pueblo next to Albuquerque.
YSLETA DEL SUR (Is-LET-ta del Sur). Down by El Paso.

One way to tell where a pot was made is to turn it over. Potters started signing pieces in the 1920s, either with their own names or the names of their pueblos. The signature didn't become universal until the 1970s, and if you learn a bit about which pueblos started signing when, the presence or absence of a signature tells you something about when the pot was made.

This list covers pretty much every place where potters have worked in the Southwest lately. Of course, over the last two thousand years, there have been others as well. On the next pages, we'll show a few pieces by prehistoric people like the Anasazi, Mogollon, and Hohokam. Potterymaking may have been a more serious business back then, but the old guys made quite a few things that fit right into our just-for-fun categories.

Have a look.

Rattle, Acoma, ca. 1950;
refrigerator magnet, Acoma, 1997;
Route 66 jar, Pauline Adson, Navajo, 1997

☀ AROUND THE HOUSE
The Dinner Table

The easiest place to start. From the beginning, long before the 650-year-old bowl in the picture on the right saw the light of day, the Indians of the Southwest made pottery for storing and eating food. Jars, bowls, plates, and pitchers aren't hard to find. In fact, they're about *all* you'll find easily, since they represent about 95 percent of Southwestern pottery.

Because so much of this ware falls roughly into the dinnerware category, there are countless ways to collect it. You can try for place settings of one type, as in the picture below. Or you can collect a single utensil: plates, cups, pitchers, salt and pepper shakers, whatever. (You probably won't bother collecting bowls—they're too easy.) Think of the picture at right as a sampler. Almost anything in it could start a narrower collection.

A word of caution: because they're unglazed, don't treat these pieces like commercial tableware and expect them to hold up. Knives scratch, water discolors, grease stains. Look, hold, enjoy—but don't put food on them.

RIGHT: *1) Salado, Tonto Polychrome, ca. 1350; 2) Navajo, 1996; 3) Jicarilla Apache, Tammie Allen, 1994; 4) Santo Domingo, Andrew Calabaza and Vicki Tenorio, 1993; 5) San Ildefonso, Tonita Roybal, ca. 1940; 6) Sandia, John Montoya, 1996; 7) Santa Clara, ca. 1940; 8) Acoma, ca. 1930; 9) Maricopa, ca. 1900; 10) Santo Domingo, Andrew Pacheco, 1996; 11) Acoma, ca. 1950; 12) Hopi, Laura Tomosie, 1950; 13) Acoma, Donna Reano, 1994; 14) Santo Domingo, ca. 1930. The diameter of the ancient bowl at the top (#1) is 13½″. BELOW: 15) Santa Clara, Earline Youngblood Tafoya, 1992; 16) Santa Clara, ca. 1935; 17) dish, Santa Clara, ca. 1940; salt bowl, Santa Clara, ca. 1955; 18) Hopi, ca. 1915; 19) dinner plate, Santa Clara, Flora Naranjo, ca. 1945; small plate, Santa Clara, ca. 1965. The dinner plate is 10¾″ in diameter.*

Coffee Break

The basic office coffee mug goes back a thousand years. If you don't believe us, look at #2. The Anasazi made them, and the Indians of the Southwest have made them for tourists for more than a hundred years. The railroad came through Arizona and New Mexico in 1880, and the souvenir market has flourished ever since.

However, we'd advise not using them for what they look like they were made for. There's one piece of technical information we can't repeat too often: *it isn't glazed*. No matter how shiny and dishwasher-safe it may look, that shine comes only from polish. This caution applies especially to the highly prized (and often highly priced) modern blackware from Santa Clara and San Ildefonso, such as the black platter on the previous page. Its beautiful color comes from a low-temperature firing, and, as we learned the hard way from a roof leak, some modern ware can be distressingly water-soluble.

Not all blackware is as fragile. Before 1920, Santa Clara potters made large black water jugs that were perfectly serviceable storage jars. The old sugar and creamer in the picture would probably hold cream just fine, but don't let anything newer get wet. Most of those fancy black pots were made for tourists and collectors to admire, not to use, and especially not for fresh flowers.

There's another even more water-threatened—and even less user-friendly—ware in the picture. The brightly colored cup and saucer from Tesuque may look just fine, but this is unfired pottery decorated with poster paint. If your hands are sweating a little, you can't even touch these pieces without smearing them. Unless, of course, they've had the benefit of modern technology. To the dismay of purists everywhere, Tesuque and Jemez poster-paint potters discovered some years back that a nice fat squirt from a spray can of fixative helped a lot, at least with the touching part.

RIGHT: *1) Zuni, ca. 1880; 2) Anasazi, Mesa Verde Black-on-white, ca. 1100; 3) Maricopa, ca. 1900; 4) Navajo, Ida Sahmie, 1994; 5) Mojave, Betty Barrackman, 1997; 6 and 7) Santa Clara, ca. 1910; 8 and 9) Santa Clara, ca. 1955; 10) Zuni, ca. 1890; 11) Isleta, ca. 1925; 12) Mogollon, Puerco Black-on-white, ca. 1050; 13) Hopi, Grace Chapella, ca. 1940; 14) Tesuque, c. 1950. The sugar and creamer from Santa Clara (#8 and #9) are both 3˝ in diameter. The Anasazi mug (#2) is big enough for a Texas-sized caffeine jolt.*

Pitchers

These go all the way back as well. Almost at the beginning of pottery history, someone figured out that if you put a handle on a jar, you could pour out of it more easily. Ever since, pitchers have come in all sizes, shapes, and colors, and gathering an assortment of them won't prove difficult.

If you want your assortment to start with those prehistoric beginnings, however, it's time to raise a red flag. This book may be mostly for fun, but one serious point needs a big fat underscore. If you're interested in buying anything prehistoric, you need to know how *not* to buy it.

For most of this century, archeologists have fought against pothunters who dig up archeological sites and destroy their scientific and historic value, and Native Americans have fought desecration of their ancestral lands and gravesites. The government has passed tough laws to stop digging on public, reservation, and, in some cases, even private land and to discourage trade in illegally dug artifacts. During the 1990s, government agencies put teeth in the law with searches and stings, and many dealers who once sold prehistoric pieces have stopped carrying them.

Some rules to live by: *don't buy prehistoric pieces off the street and don't buy them without documentation that attests to their source and legal status.* Buy them in the open market at stores, shows, or auctions from known, reputable dealers; pay with a check or credit card; and be sure you get—and keep—all the paperwork.

ABOVE AND RIGHT: *1) Mogollon, Puerco Black-on-white, ca. 1050; 2) Anasazi, Mancos Corrugated, ca. 1100; 3) Hohokam, Casa Grande Red-on-buff, ca. 1200; 4) Santo Domingo, ca. 1940; 5) Picuris, Anthony Durand, 1992; 6) Maricopa, Mary Juan, ca. 1940; 7) Acoma, ca. 1950; 8) Santo Domingo, ca. 1930; 9) Santo Domingo, ca. 1935; 10) Jemez, ca. 1970; 11) Santa Clara, ca. 1910; 12) Navajo, Mary Henderson, ca. 1975; 13) Acoma, Mary Lewis, ca. 1990; 14) Mojave, ca. 1940; 15) Tohono O'Odham or Maricopa, ca. 1960; 16) Laguna, Evelyn Cheromiah, 1994; 17) Hopi, Joy Navasie, ca. 1945; 18) Santo Domingo, ca. 1920; 19) Santa Clara, ca. 1940; 20) Santo Domingo, Hilda Coriz, 1992; 21) Acoma, Diane Lewis, 1994; 22) Isleta, ca. 1925; 23) Acoma, Drew Lewis, 1995. The big red Santo Domingo pitcher (#4) is 9¾" high.*

Salt & Pepper

These, however, don't go very far back at all. The ancient Anasazi didn't see a need for dispensers for exotic condiments, but the tourists who arrived when the railroads came to the Southwest in the late nineteenth century were well jaded by the fripperies of European civilization. Local traders, of course, knew exactly what those tourists wanted for souvenirs. For most of the twentieth century, potters in the Southwest have turned out great quantities of whatever tourists would buy.

The pueblos nearest the railroads and the Anglo population centers caught on first. That's why you find the earliest pure tourist pottery coming from Isleta, Laguna, and from the Mojaves, who took advantage of nearby stops on the Santa Fe's cross-country line. Tesuque and Cochiti, the nearest pueblos to the city of Santa Fe and therefore probably the worldliest, were in at the beginning as well.

By 1900, perhaps ten different groups were industriously cranking out tourist ware in quality that ranged from fancy to slapdash. Maricopa and Pima potters had an outlet in Phoenix, and the "Chili Line," the branch of the Denver and Rio Grande that connected Santa Fe to Española, brought Santa Clara into the marketplace. Zuni was the nearest pottery resource to the railroad town of Gallup, and Acoma, a much larger pueblo, was right across the tracks from the station at Laguna. Other pueblos joined in later, and by the 1920s, Hopi, Zia, Santo Domingo, and almost every other pottery-producing pueblo and rancheria was eager for the tourist dollar. Jemez and San Juan joined the parade in the 1930s, and everybody else on our pottery map has been in and out of the market since.

As far as salt and pepper shakers go, we're sure they appeared at the beginning of the tourist days, but our own collection seems largely stuck in a single period. Based on our highly incomplete research (and still-developing acquisition program), we're placing the Golden Age of salt and pepper shakers at right around 1950.

RIGHT: *1) Maricopa, ca. 1940; 2) Hopi, Nellie Douma, ca. 1960; 3) Santa Clara, ca. 1950; 4) Hopi, ca. 1925; 5) Tesuque, ca. 1950; 6) Zia, ca. 1945; 7) Jemez, ca. 1960; 8) Jemez, ca. 1950; 9) Jemez, ca. 1955. The tray holding the red Santa Clara pair (#3) is 5½˝ wide.*

Ladles

Everybody makes these, but they've been a Hopi specialty forever.
If our salt-and-pepper-shaker collection seems to have stuck itself at a single time, our scoop-and-ladle collection seems to tilt heavily towards a single place.

The oldest pieces on the right-hand page—the red-on-buff Hohokam scoop (#8) and the two black-on-white Anasazi ladles (#9 and #11)—date from before the pueblos at Hopi were built, but the Anasazi ones came from the Four Corners area in southeast Colorado and were made by the people who most likely populated the Hopi mesas a couple of centuries after they made the ladles. As for the rest of the array, seven of the nine remaining pieces are from Hopi, with dates ranging from A.D. 1300 to 1997.

Ladles started out like simple scoops, like the Hohokam piece, but they had an interesting second phase in their development. Gourds were common in the Southwest, and early inhabitants probably used them as containers long before they started making pottery. One fact that makes this a reasonably safe bet is that much of the earliest pottery mimicked gourd shapes. The shape of Anasazi ladle #11 holds no mystery whatever if you think of it as half a gourd.

For the last thousand years plus, ladles have mostly been bowls with handles, usually pierced for hanging from a thong or a string, like most of the ones in this picture. Hopi potter Jean Sahmie's piece from 1997 (#6) calls for special mention. It's clearly a ladle, but it's also a beautifully comfortable sculpture in the best tradition of contemporary art, and, at the same time, a sophisticated cartoon. The traditional hair rolls on either side of the handle define it as a portrait of a Hopi maiden, and the mischievously placed hanging hole gives her a vacant, slack-jawed attitude that makes us cherish the piece even more.

RIGHT: *1) Detail of Jean Sahmie's ladle (#6); 2) Hopi, Jeddito Black-on-yellow, ca. 1300; 3) Tesuque, Priscilla Vigil, ca. 1975; 4) Hopi, ca. 1935; 5) Hopi, ca. 1945; 6) Hopi, Jean Sahmie, 1997; 7) Hopi, ca. 1950; 8) Hohokam, Sacaton Red-on-buff, ca. 1050; 9) Anasazi, McElmo Black-on-white, ca. 800; 10) Hopi, Tusayan Polychrome, ca. 1350; 11) Anasazi, Mesa Verde Black-on-white, ca. 950; 12) Zuni, Chris Nastario, 1994; 13) Hopi, ca. 1940. The big McElmo ladle (#9) is 11″ long.*

1

ARIZONA HISTORICAL SOCIETY
LIBRARY

ALBUQUERQUE ACADEMY
LIBRARY

19

Candlesticks

Think of a shape, and they've made a candlestick to match it. Tall
ones, squatty ones, round ones, square ones, twisted ones, ones that look like
shoes, ones that look like birds, ones that just look odd. They're all usable. In
fact, we had to clean wax off most of the ones we found.

The ones in the picture are all products of the tourist age. The people of
the pre-Spanish Southwest may have had little use for salt and pepper shakers,
but seed jars with single small dispenser holes served a similar function.
Candles, however, weren't part of their technology.

We've never seen a candleholder made before 1880, the date railroads
came through. It's easy to conclude that Indian potters never made any until
the traders pointed out their marketability. Yet Europeans lived among the
Pueblos from 1600 on, and Europeans used candles. Of course, they used
candlesticks of metal and wood, more durable than pottery, and they
imported wares from Spain, Mexico, and beyond, but they also recognized the
skills of the native potters. As early as 1581, the Portuguese explorer Hernan
Gallegos wrote, *"These vessels are so excellent and delicate that the process of
manufacture is worth watching; for they equal, and even surpass, the pottery
made in Portugal."* Contemporary Spanish accounts indicated that pueblo
potters made utilitarian pottery for the settlers as well as for themselves, and
anything the Spanish needed. If they made candlesticks,
salt shakers, and the like, these pieces have disappeared,
perhaps regarded as no more valuable than we regard a
paper plate or a plastic cup.

The pieces in the picture barely scratch the surface.
Collectors have treasured these candleholders for years,
and, if you want to go after them, you'll have to compete.
The only reason we found something as rare, wonderful
and peculiar as #6 is that we got there first. It turned up in an
antique store and never reached the channels that pottery collectors frequent.

ABOVE AND RIGHT: *1) Santa Clara (pair), ca. 1910; 2) Santa Clara, ca. 1930; 3) Santa Clara (pair), ca. 1972; 4) Zuni,
ca. 1900; 5) Santa Clara (pair), Ramona Suina, ca. 1950; 6) Tesuque, Juan and Lorencita Pino, ca. 1940; 7) Hopi, ca. 1940;
8) Mata Ortiz, Naty Ortega, 1997; 9) San Ildefonso (pair), Dolores Gonzales, ca. 1950; 10) Santo Domingo, ca. 1965;
11) Maricopa, ca. 1925; 12) Acoma, ca. 1950; 13) Tohono O'Odham, ca. 1930; 14) San Ildefonso (pair), Carmelita Dunlap,
ca. 1950; 15) Santo Domingo, ca. 1925. Juan and Lorencita Pino's technicolor effort (#6) is 6″ high.*

Canteens

If there's one thing that's always been important to the Southwest, it's water. Canteens and other water-carrying vessels, large and small, have been part of the potter's vocabulary from the beginning.

They're also still very much with us. Three of the canteens on these pages date from 1996 and 1997, and all three followed traditional forms. The three canteens on this page tell their own story of continuity. The Tularosa canteen from 1200 (#3) and the Acoma parrot canteen from 1940 (#2) aren't all that different in shape. That parrot has a lot of tradition as well. Parrots and their feathers were traded into the Southwest from Mexico more than a thousand years ago, and they show up on prehistoric pottery in abstract form. Parrots appeared on large Acoma jars in the nineteenth century, and they're still with us (#1 is a large canteen from 1997).

Perhaps because water is so important to the Southwest, canteens don't seem to show the same level of whimsy that some of the other forms exhibit. Birds, bears, and turtles decorate them, but not particularly lightheartedly. Instead, these canteens have serious, almost ritualized designs that seldom break out of the constraints imposed by tradition. This circumspect approach shows through whether the canteen is carefully crafted by highly regarded potters as an important piece, like Arthur and Hilda Coriz's #10, or produced as an inexpensive curio by potters who decorate precast pottery for quick sale to tourists, like #12.

ABOVE AND RIGHT: *1) Acoma, Drew Lewis, 1997; 2) Acoma, ca. 1940; 3) Mogollon, Tularosa Black-on-white, ca. 1200; 4) Acoma, Jessie Louis, ca. 1965; 5) Acoma, ca. 1920; 6) Acoma, ca. 1955; 7) Isleta, Diane Wade, 1997; 8) Tohono O'Odham, ca. 1975; 9) Zia, Seferina Bell, ca. 1955; 10) Santo Domingo, Arthur and Hilda Coriz, 1996; 11) Acoma, C. Maurus Chino, 1987; 12) Laguna, D. and M. Pasquale, 1992; 13) Acoma, ca. 1965; 14) Santa Ana, Lena Garcia, ca. 1980; 15) Hopi, ca. 1950; 16) Zia, Gloria Gachupin, ca. 1990; 17) Santo Domingo, Hilda Tenorio (Coriz), ca. 1985; 18) Hopi, ca. 1935; 19) Acoma, Ergil Vallo, ca. 1985. Drew Lewis's big parrot jar (#1) is 9¼" high, and Seferina Bell's red Zia canteen (#9) is 8" high.*

Wedding Vases

Sometimes Life Imitates Art. A friend of ours recently sent us a clipping from the Santa Fe *New Mexican*, a wedding-article-with-picture like we've all seen again and again in our own local paper. It describes how the bride and groom drank from a traditional black wedding vase "made by the groom's mother, a famous potter, and fired three days before the ceremony."

That potter was Toni Roller of the Tafoya family, famous for its unflinching adherence to purely traditional pottery standards, and the fact that she made one for her son's wedding speaks volumes about how important the wedding vase is to Santa Clara's pottery tradition. Betty LeFree's scholarly *Santa Clara Pottery Today*, written in 1975, offers a recounting of the tradition by potter Teresita Naranjo, but it also suggests that around 1900, John Candelario of Santa Fe's Original Curio Shop invented the shape for Santa Clara potters and fabricated a whole "wedding vase" tradition to convince tourists that they were buying pottery steeped in history.

If that's true, Candelario had a defense. Double-spouted vases appeared in pre-Columbian Mexico, and nineteenth-century anthropologists thought the Pueblo Indians were direct descendants of the Aztecs and Toltecs. It was a short leap to conclude that Mexican pre-Columbian pottery was ancestral ware for the locals. Maps of the Southwest echo that thinking in prehistoric site names: "Montezuma's Castle," "Aztec Ruins," "Montezuma's Well."

Whether Candelario invented it or not, the form is now made by every pottery-producing pueblo, is an appropriate wedding gift, and, according to the *New Mexican*, is used ceremonially by the people who should know best. Any day, we'll see one on top of a wedding cake.

RIGHT: *1) Jemez, Santana Seonia, 1997; 2) Hopi, Maynard and Veronica Navasie, 1995; 3) Navajo, Elizabeth Manygoats, 1996; 4) Taos, Mariancita G., 1995; 5) Zuni, Dedrick and Lorenda Cellicon, 1996; 6) Mata Ortiz, Martin Olmos, 1995; 7) Hopi, Gloria Kahe, 1996; 8) Acoma, Stella Shutiva, ca. 1980; 9) Jemez, Geraldine Sandia, 1996; 10) Hopi, Vernida Nampeyo, 1995; 11) Tohono O'Odham, Angea, ca. 1990; 12) Jemez, Pauline Romero, 1992; 13) Laguna, Andrew Padilla, 1994; 14) Acoma, Juana Leno, ca. 1960; 15) Navajo, Elizabeth Manygoats, 1997; 16) Isleta, ca. 1925; 17) Tesuque, ca. 1975; 18) Santa Clara, Teresa Gutierrez, 1996; 19) Jemez, Chinana, ca. 1980; 20) Mata Ortiz, Anita Trillo, 1995; 21) Acoma, ca. 1940; 22) Maricopa, ca. 1940. Maynard and Veronica Navasie's #2 is 13¼" high. Santana Seonia's #1, which looks like it actually does belong on a cake, is 6¼" high.*

1

25

Smoking Paraphernalia

The Indians on the East Coast introduced Sir Walter Raleigh to tobacco. In the Southwest, they cashed in on it for years. It didn't take long for ashtrays to become the number one tourist souvenir item in Southwestern pottery. The earliest example in the picture at right dates from 1910, a time when smoking was still pretty much a male pastime. But right after World War I and into the 1950s, the cigarette was a symbol of emancipated sophistication for men and women alike. By 1950, America's idea of the well-equipped home had ashtrays in every room and a table lighter on the coffee table. Blue Corn's table lighter (#12) was a meticulously finished item that represented the highest level of pottery prestige: San Ildefonso blackware in the manner of the legendary Maria Martinez.

Pueblo potters cranked out ashtrays by the hundreds from the 1920s through the 1960s, and they're not rare today, despite a fatal flaw in their manufacture. Unfortunately, extinguishing a cigarette on unglazed pottery makes a permanent smudge.

The large number of Southwestern Indian ashtrays still around speaks to their original quantity of manufacture, not their durability. We suspect the reason that second-hand stores aren't piled high with them is simply that thousands of homemakers who tried to wash them ultimately gave up and threw them away.

Although the potters made their ashtrays to be used, it's hard to believe that the potters who made smoking pipes ever thought anyone would actually smoke anything in them. This might explain why potters still make them in these days when much of America seems determined to eradicate smoking. The pipe that makes fun of a Spanish dignitary came from Isleta in the 1930s, the blackware one from Santa Clara (#12) dates from the 1970s, and the one from Zuni (#6) and the outlandish one from Isleta (#8) come from the 1990s.

RIGHT: *1) Maricopa, ca. 1925; 2) Acoma, ca. 1930; 3) Maricopa, ca. 1930; 4) Santa Clara, Margaret Naranjo, 1956; 5) Zuni, Priscilla Peynetsa, 1994; 6) Tesuque, ca. 1910; 7) Santa Clara, ca. 1940; 8) Isleta, Chapa, 1997; 9) Hopi, ca. 1960; 10) Santa Clara, ca. 1975; 11) Acoma, ca. 1930; 12) San Ildefonso, Blue Corn, ca. 1970; 13) Isleta, ca. 1935; 14) Isleta, ca. 1925; 15) Maricopa, Claudia Kavoka, ca. 1940; 16) Laguna, ca. 1935; 17) Maricopa, ca. 1940; 18) Maricopa, ca. 1930. Priscilla Peynetsa's pipe (#6) is 8" long. The old Tesuque piece with the women grinding corn (#5) is 6" in diameter.*

1

2

3

6

5

4

7

8

9

10

11

12

13

14

15

16

17

18

27

☀ USEFUL THINGS
Baskets

Everybody knows what you mean when you talk about an "Indian Basket." Except that it's occasionally a pot. Like the pitcher, the basket goes back to the earliest days of prehistoric pottery. Fastidious archeologists prefer words like "bowl with strap handle" to describe these creations, but they were pottery baskets, just like the ones in the picture.

For more than a century, pottery baskets have been big at Zuni, both in ritual form and as a tourist item. The prayer meal basket with its dragonfly and tadpole water symbols held cornmeal for religious ceremonies, but not necessarily always. Zuni has never been rigid about the use of its pottery, and these baskets have been made by the hundreds, some for ceremony, some for sale. More than likely, some were used ceremonially and then sold. Jennie Laate's #11 looks almost exactly like one pictured in the 1880–1881 annual report of the Bureau of Ethnology. There's no ceremony that we know of attached to #19, however. It's just plain eccentric, which makes it an ideal candidate for this book.

If Zuni created the earliest tourist baskets, Isleta made an industry of them. During the first third of the twentieth century, Isleta potters turned out hundreds and probably thousands of brightly colored little baskets with rope handles like #5, #7, #8, and #10, and potters at Laguna, Acoma, and perhaps even Zuni copied the form.

At Santa Clara, they took the Isleta twisted handle and gentrified it, making enough solid "engagement baskets" like #4 and #12 to create yet another tradition.

Meanwhile, other souvenir-producing places like San Juan and Maricopa turned out the occasional simple basket, and Mojave and Quechan produced fanciful ones. Santo Domingo created its own form, a hybrid shape the people who write books have never quite figured out what to call. Is it a basket? Is it a double-spouted pitcher? Or is it simply what the archeologists seem to prefer—just another variation of a bowl with strap handle? Look at #1, then decide for yourself.

RIGHT: 1) Santo Domingo, Robert Tenorio, 1995; 2) Acoma, ca. 1935; 3) Acoma, Dorothy Patricio, 1991; 4) Santa Clara, Reycita Naranjo, 1984; 5) Isleta, ca. 1925; 6) Acoma, ca. 1950; 7) Isleta, ca. 1925; 8) Isleta, ca. 1925; 9) Mojave, ca. 1925; 10) Isleta, ca. 1925; 11) Zuni, Jennie Laate, ca. 1980; 12) Santa Clara, Mae Tapia, ca. 1980; 13) Laguna, 1931; 14) Santa Clara, Carol Velarde, 1994; 15) Acoma, ca. 1965; 16) Hopi, ca. 1925; 17) Tesuque, ca. 1910; 18) Laguna, ca. 1930; 19) Zuni, ca. 1900. Robert Tenorio's big double-spouted pitcher basket (#1) is 9½" wide.

Moccasins

For reasons we can't explain, everybody makes these, and they made them long before there were tourists buying cute souvenirs.
Anthropologists have suggested all kinds of reasons why the Anasazi, the Mogollon, and their contemporaries made pottery shaped like boots and shoes. Little shoe-shaped pieces with handles like #2 might have been water-sippers for infants. When the Anasazi made larger plainware pieces shaped like #1, they could have used them as warming bowls, the theory being that you stuck the toe near the fire and drank or ate from the cooler heel—a speculation that we've read on little display cards at two eminent museums.

1

2

Whatever the impulse that drove their manufacture, these pottery moccasins never went away. We've heard suggestions that they had mysterious ceremonial uses at different times in different places, yet it's hard to feel that about any of the pieces in the pictures. The thousand-year-old Mogollon piece (#2) aside, the rest of these appear to have been made for fun, and even that ancient example doesn't strike us as a highly serious effort.

At Zuni, they made them anatomically correct, meticulously allowing the correct amount of space for toes, insteps, and ankle bones. At Maricopa, they made them as traditional moccasins. They also made them as your great-grandfather's high-top oxfords and as silly little ashtrays. At Hopi, they made them in careful conformance with the pottery styles of the day. At Cochiti and Santo Domingo, they made each more imaginatively than the next. At San Juan, they made them red. At Santa Clara, they made them black. At Acoma, they made some strange ones. And at Isleta, they made as many as they could.

How many did they all make? There are thirty-three shoes on these pages, and they represent only about a third of what we've accumulated over the past few years. If this sample means anything, they made a lot.

RIGHT: *1) Hopi, ca. 1895; 2) Mogollon, Reserve Black-on-white, ca. 1025; 3) Cochiti, ca. 1890; 4) Zuni, ca. 1900; 5) Zuni, ca. 1890; 6) San Juan, ca. 1920; 7) Hopi, ca. 1960; 8) Cochiti or Santo Domingo, ca. 1950; 9) Cochiti or Santo Domingo, ca. 1920; 10) Isleta, ca. 1915; 11) Maricopa, ca. 1950 (pair); 12) Taos, ca. 1980; 13) Maricopa, ca. 1920 (pair); 14) Cochiti, ca. 1960 (pair); 15) Cochiti, ca. 1935; 16) Acoma, Shdiya'aits'a (Gertrude Poncho), 1995; 17) Santo Domingo, ca. 1920; 18) Laguna, ca. 1925 (pair); 19) Santa Clara, ca. 1970; 20) Santo Domingo, ca. 1900; 21) Isleta, ca. 1910 (pair); 22) Maricopa, Claudia Kavoka, ca. 1950; 23) Maricopa, Lena Mesquerre, ca. 1935 (pair); 24) Maricopa, ca. 1940; 25) Maricopa, ca. 1930 (pair). The tall old Cochiti boot (#3) is 6¾" high; the Hopi piece on this page (#1) is 5¾" long.*

3

4

5

6

7

8

9

10

11

12

13

14

15

16

17

18

19

20

21

22

23

24

25

31

✳ SMALL PEOPLE
Figurines

In Southwestern pottery, human figurines were scarce until the nineteenth century. Then the traders got to Cochiti. The origin of the Cochiti figurine may be similar to the rumored origin of the wedding vase—traders representing pre-Columbian Mexican figurines to Cochiti potters as their supposedly ancestral pottery and asking for more.

We know for sure, based on well-known and well-documented photographs of Santa Fe traders' arrays taken in the 1880s, that Cochiti and, to a lesser degree, Tesuque and Zuni potters were producing quirky figurines for tourist sale, and that they were being offered as "Montezuma" (*i.e.*, "prehistoric") pottery. Why Cochiti in particular? Bob Gallegos, an expert on historic pottery, has a plausible explanation. It's close to Santa Fe, just a few miles farther away than Tesuque, which sits on Santa Fe's outskirts. And it's right next to Peña Blanca, a Hispanic town that in the 1870s offered convenient rowdy saloons and worldly pleasures. Quite simply, Cochiti potters were more sophisticated about city ways than their counterparts in other pueblos, and better prepared to make some money by caricaturing the non-Indians around them.

Around the same time, a circus came through, giving the potters even more fuel for fancy. Quickly, Cochiti figurines assumed a grotesque but engaging personality unique to themselves. Today, the tradition still exists at Cochiti, as exemplified by the work of Virgil Ortiz (#1 and #2). It also exists all over the rest of the the Southwest, from Santa Clara to Hopi to Maricopa, and at places in between.

RIGHT: *1) Cochiti, Virgil Ortiz, 1992; 2) Cochiti, Virgil Ortiz, 1996; 3) Maricopa, Vesta Bread, ca. 1950; 4) Cochiti, Louis and Virginia Naranjo, 1996; 5) Tesuque, Manuel Vigil, ca. 1960; 6) Cochiti, Ivan Lewis, 1990; 7) Navajo, Dennis John, 1996; 8) Hopi, Loren Nampeyo, 1993; 9) Tesuque, probably Manuel Vigil, ca. 1960; 10) Cochiti, Helen Cordero, ca. 1980; 11) Santa Clara, Gary Gutierrez, 1996; 12) Cochiti, Dorothy Trujillo, ca. 1965; 13) Tesuque, probably Manuel Vigil, ca. 1960; 14) Santa Clara, Gary Gutierrez, 1993; 15) Santa Clara, Gary Gutierrez, 1996; 16) Santa Clara, Dorothy and Paul Gutierrez, 1993; 17) Cochiti, Martha Arquero, 1997; 18) Jemez, Cheryl Fragua, 1997 (set of 3); 19) Cochiti, Seferina Ortiz, 1994; 20) Santa Clara, Stephanie Naranjo, 1994; 21) Santa Clara, Gary Gutierrez, 1993; 22) Santa Clara, Stephanie Naranjo, 1994. The giant Virgil Ortiz Pueblo Dandy on this page is 21" high, and Vesta Bread's tall Maricopa effigy jar (#3) is 14" high.*

Storytellers

Another Cochiti invention, and one potter gets the credit. In 1964, a potter named Helen Cordero never could quite get the hang of making round pots, so Juanita Arquero, her in-law and teacher, suggested she try figurines. She made a few moderately successful efforts, nativity scenes and traditional Cochiti mother-and-child figurines called "singing mothers." When a collector asked for a singing mother with multiple children, she gave him a figure she called a "storyteller," based on a memory of her grandfather surrounded by children as he told his tales. (The storyteller's origin has been retold so often that it leaves an impression of her grandfather as a stereotypical sweet old grandpa. Santiago Quintana was far more than that. He was a historic figure, Cochiti's first celebrity, mentioned and quoted in half a dozen books written between 1890 and 1930. He guided Adolph Bandelier to the Anasazi ruins near Santa Fe that became a national monument bearing Bandelier's name.)

The storyteller caught on immediately, and within months, Helen was working full time turning them out for the collector's market. Her first storyteller held five children, but the more she added, the more attention they received. The race to create the ultimate storyteller reached ridiculous proportions, and potters have produced efforts with more than two hundred little creatures sitting about—an infestation rather than a visit.

Serious or not, the storyteller and the singing mother have been staple items ever since. The first Jemez storytellers appeared in 1968. In the mid-1980s, there were sixty Jemez potters making them, and at one point there may have been as many as a hundred. The Teller family from Isleta was in full storyteller production by the 1980s. By the mid-1990s, the craze appeared to have peaked, but it's far from over.

The storyteller will be with us for years to come.

ABOVE AND RIGHT: *1) Jemez, Chris Fragua, 1992; 2) Acoma, Judy Lewis, 1996; 3) Cochiti, Mary and Leonard Trujillo, 1996; 4) Isleta, Chris Teller, 1993; 5) Cochiti, Louis and Virginia Naranjo, 1995; 6) Jemez, Caroline Seonia, 1996; 7) Cochiti, Louis and Virginia Naranjo, 1995; 8) Cochiti, Louise Suina, ca. 1980; 9) Cochiti, Denise Suina, 1993; 10) Cochiti, Felicita Eustace, 1996; 11) Jemez, Lucero Gachupin, 1994; 12) Jemez, F. Fragua, 1993; 13) Cochiti, Marie Suina, ca. 1970; 14) Acoma, Judy Lewis, 1996; 15) Cochiti, Rose Brown, 1996; 16) Santa Clara, Margaret and Luther Gutierrez, ca. 1970; 17) Santa Clara, Dorothy and Paul Gutierrez, 1992; 18) Isleta, Robin Teller, 1992; 19) Jemez, P. Toya, 1996; 20) Cheyenne/Cochiti, Margaret Quintana, 1993; 21) Jemez, J. L. Fragua, 1993; 22) Jemez, F. Fragua, 1993; 23) Jemez, A. Toya, ca. 1980; 24) Jemez, Joyce Lucero, 1997. Chris Fragua's reclining koshare (#1) with the cowboy and the Indian on board is 8½″ long, and Denia Suina's #9 is 6¾″ high.*

35

Nacimientos

These are a latter-day phenomenon, and when you stop to think about it, "phenomenon" isn't too strong a word. What makes the *nacimiento*, or nativity set, unusual is that it represents the first widespread, unashamedly Christian art ever made by the Native Americans of the Southwest. Pueblo silversmiths had made necklaces with pendant crosses, which pleased the Catholic fathers, but the double Cross of Lorraine also served well as a dragonfly symbol in their own religion.

But in the late 1950s, Tesuque's Manuel Vigil (see page 33 for some of his work) began making folk-art, poster-painted nativity sets. It took another ten years before other pueblos followed. The ones that followed, and the ones that have produced the great bulk of nativity sets since, had all made pottery figu-rines for years. Manuel Vigil's Tesuque had produced rain gods since the nine-teenth century, Cochiti had made its human figurines, and Santa Clara had been making its *animalitos,* whimsical little animal figurines, for almost as long.

By the end of the 1960s, Frances Suina, Helen Cordero, Dorothy Trujillo, and Felipa Trujillo of Cochiti were making nativity sets, and the Gutierrezes of Santa Clara—Margaret and Luther, Dorothy and Paul— followed within a few months. Other pueblos made them as well. There's a very early set from Acoma to the right and, on the next page, a recent set from Nambé. The Nambé set indicated to us that, even with a one hundred–percent Christian item like the *nacimiento*, the Christianization of the pueblos remains less than complete. When we talked to Robert Vigil before he made the set, he asked us whether we wanted the "Arab version or the Corn Mother version." Since we already had some of the former, we voted for the latter. As luck would have it, two buffaloes and the Corn Mother didn't make it through the firing. Even without her presence, however, the message is clear. In this *nacimiento*, there's no question about the pure Southwestern origin of the animal population.

ABOVE AND RIGHT: *1) Acoma, probably Ethel Shields, ca. 1975; 2) Santa Clara, Dorothy and Paul Gutierrez, 1992; 3) Cochiti, Josephine Arquero, ca. 1985; 4) Nambé, Robert Vigil, 1995. Josephine Arquero's presiding angel is 4⅛″ tall, while the infant in the Acoma set on this page is barely an inch long.*

Rain Gods & Other Deities

The rain god has a long and sacred tradition, mostly made up by a trader named Jake Gold. Figurative pottery in the American Southwest goes back to the beginning, but it reached its first real popularity about 1300 in the Casas Grandes culture, centered in Chihuahua, Mexico, seventy miles south of New Mexico's bootheel. They made what the scholars call "hooded effigies," jars like #2 and #4, which have a certain godlike—or at least, not-like-the-rest-of-us—air about them.

Despite the nineteenth-century Maricopa version in the picture on the right (#6), the hooded effigy all but vanished for the next few hundred years, and most Southwestern potters stopped making pottery images of gods. The Mojaves made four-spouted effigy jars like #14 and #17 and dolls that looked a lot like ones the Hohokam had made a thousand years before, but production was small and isolated. Until recent potters began creating kachina forms and recreating prehistoric shapes, modern Southwestern figurative pottery consisted mostly of recognizable humans and known animals.

For a hundred years, however, the Tesuque rain god had a large number of people thinking otherwise. These E.T.-like figures (#1, #7, #8, #9, #10, #11, #13, and #15 are all examples) first appeared in the 1870s, and a Santa Fe trader named Jake Gold made sure that there were enough to satisfy tourists looking for authentic Indian sacred items. He sold them for $6.50 a barrel in 1905, and a Chicago candy company gave them away as a premium. They were the furthest thing from fine pottery, usually unfired, often decorated in inks and later in poster paints, and made in great quantities into the 1930s. They never did vanish entirely, as the later examples in the picture demonstrate.

Our most bizarre rain god is #1, which pretends to be the most sacred of all. It's one of the poorer unfired, undecorated examples, but during the psychedelic 1960s, someone gave him a rawhide cape, put burnt offerings and a feather in his rain bucket, and glued him to a three-level plinth so he can preside forever over the lesser gods around him.

RIGHT: *1) Tesuque, c. 1965; 2) Chihuahua, Villa Ahumada Polychrome, ca. 1400; 3) Mata Ortiz, Juan Quezada, 1975; 4) Chihuahua, Madera Red, ca. 1350; 5) Hopi, Darlene Vigil Nampeyo, 1996; 6) Maricopa, ca. 1870; 7) Tesuque, Ignacia Duran, 1992; 8) Tesuque, ca. 1910; 9) Tesuque, ca. 1920; 10) Tesuque, c. 1975; 11) Tesuque, ca. 1900; 12) Tesuque, Ka'Ween, 1988; 13) Tesuque, ca. 1920; 14) Mojave, ca. 1920; 15) Tesuque, Renee Herrera, 1996; 16) Maricopa, Dorothea Sunn, 1997; 17) Mojave, ca. 1880. The rain god with the top hat (#8) is 7½″ high.*

✳ CREATURES
Bears

Man and bear have an ancient affinity. As long as what we think of
bears comes from what we see in magazine pictures and TV footage, they
don't seem much different from big cuddly dogs. That's why park rangers
have to remind tourists to stay clear of them in order to avoid being eaten. We
grow up with teddy bears, and in the urbanized United States, it's hard to see
bears as a threat.

But Pueblo Indians lived—and many still live—on the edge of wilderness.
Romanticized perceptions of bears should have no place in their culture, yet
the Indians of the Southwest seem always to have had a cordial coexistence
with fearsome creatures. Spiders and snakes decorate Maricopa, Tohono
O'Odham, Hopi, and Acoma pottery, and at Santa Clara, the pueblo that
produces the most high-end pottery, the bear appears everywhere.

The bear paw symbol (a curved smile line with three tick marks over it,
like this: ᐎ) shows up again and again on Santa Clara pottery because, we're
told, a bear led the people to water during a period of drought and starvation.
Animal figurines and bears have been a major part of Santa Clara's pottery
production for the last hundred years, and whimsical little black, red, and
polychrome *animalitos* not only abound in our collections, they proliferate.

The picture on the right shows eight very different Santa Clara bears. But
it also shows single figures and storytellers from Cochiti, San Ildefonso,
Jemez, Laguna, Taos, and Zuni. All, like Santa Clara, are situated near enough
to the mountains for residents to be quite conscious of the fact that bears can
be scary as well as cute.

Jack Kalestewa's Zuni bear (#4) has a traditional Zuni design element, the
heartline, a jagged line extending from the mouth to the heart, unblocked so
the animal can breathe. When the Zuni depict a bear or a deer to be hunted,
the heart line serves as both a respectful tribute to the spirit of the animal and
a talisman of luck for the hunter.

RIGHT: *1) Navajo, Louise Goodman, 1995; 2) Cochiti, Louis and Virginia Naranjo, 1996; 3) Laguna, Dennis Rodriguez,*
1996; 4) Zuni, Jack Kalestewa, 1996; 5) Cochiti, E. Herrera, 1992; 6) Acoma, Evelyn Garcia, 1989; 7) San Ildefonso, Wan
Povi (Kathy Sanchez), 1996; 8) Navajo, Jimmy Wilson, 1996; 9) Cochiti, Inez Ortiz, 1996; 10) Isleta, Scott Small, 1994;
11) Santa Clara, Dorothy and Paul Gutierrez, 1992; 12) San Juan, Alvin Curran, 1994; 13) Navajo, Lorraine Williams,
1996; 14) Santa Clara, Birdell Bourdon, 1997; 15) Taos, Paul Romero, 1996; 16) Santa Clara, Forrest and Karen Naranjo,
1993; 17) Santa Clara, Dusty Naranjo, 1993; 18) San Ildefonso, Wan Povi (Kathy Sanchez), 1993; 19) Hopi, ca. 1990;
20) Acoma, Marvis Aragon, Jr., 1992; 21) Jemez, ca. 1980; 22) Santa Clara, Forrest Naranjo, 1994; 23) Santa Clara, Bernice
Suazo, 1994; 24) Santa Clara, Margaret Gutierrez, 1993; 25) Santa Clara, Pat Tafoya, 1994. Louise Goodman's bear (#1) is
8¼" high, which isn't anywhere near as tall as some of hers. Sometimes she makes these more than 20" high.

CREATURES

Beasts, Wild & Mythical

Southwestern potters portray any and every creature, and never let little things like reality get in the way. The picture on the right shows the familiar animals of the pueblos' forests: beaver and skunk, buffalo and deer, all nicely portrayed. It also shows a few creatures no one from any pueblo has ever seen.

It was ever thus, apparently. The ancient Hohokam censer on this page has the face of a horned toad and the legs of a piano, and it stares firmly back at you like no other creature that ever existed on this planet.

A thousand years later, fantasy persists, and no one stretches the boundaries more often than the potters of Cochiti. The examples on the opposite page include imaginary beasts from both ends of the twentieth century, including a horned dragon from around 1910, and a dinosaur from the 1996 Indian Market. At Cochiti, even the familiar gets stretched. Damacia Cordero's deer is quite tame compared to her usual work, but Snowflake Flower's coyote storyteller is over the top.

1

Santa Clara's traditional blackware *animalitos* seem conventional by comparison, and Dorothy and Paul Gutierrez have made thousands of them since the 1960s. But Paul's aunt Margaret and her niece Stephanie Naranjo have a more whimsical, multicolored outlook. Mamie Deschillie's elephant, a form of Navajo folk art called a "mud toy," is even more extravagant.

There's one clear lesson in all this. A Southwestern potter doesn't need to have an elephant or a dinosaur in the back yard to know exactly what one should look like.

ABOVE AND RIGHT: *1) Hohokam, Sacaton Red-on-buff, ca. 950; 2) Cochiti, Josephine Arquero, 1996; 3) Acoma, Marie Chino, ca. 1975; 4) Cochiti, Snowflake Flower, 1992; 5) Cochiti, ca. 1910; 6) Santo Domingo, Andrew Pacheco, 1993; 7) Cochiti, Damacia Cordero, ca. 1975; 8) Navajo, Mamie Deschillie, 1995; 9) Pojoaque, Cordelia Gomez, 1993; 10) Santa Clara, Dorothy and Paul Gutierrez, 1993; 11) Navajo, 1995; 12) Santa Clara, Tony Gutierrez, 1997; 13) Santa Clara, Stephanie Naranjo, 1990; 14) Santa Clara, Paul Gutierrez, 1992; 15) Santa Clara, Dorothy and Paul Gutierrez, 1994; 16) Santa Clara, Margaret Gutierrez, 1994; 17) Santa Clara, Dorothy and Paul Gutierrez, 1993; 18) Santa Clara, ca. 1950; 19) Santa Clara, Margaret Gutierrez, 1994; 20) San Ildefonso, Louis Naranjo, 1990; 21) Santa Clara, Margaret Gutierrez, 1994; 22) Santa Clara, Dorothy and Paul Gutierrez, 1992. Snowflake Flower's coyote storyteller #4 is 7½" high. The Hohokam frog-turned-bulldog (#1) is 4⅜" long.*

Farm Animals

Yes, potters enjoy giving us exotic beasts. But they have just as much fun with the commonplace. Here, you won't find any prehistoric pieces, because before the Spanish came, these commonplace animals didn't exist in the Southwest. Domestic sheep, goats, horses, pigs, cows, and housecats all came with the European settlers, and they not only changed the lives of the potters, they changed the way they made pottery.

Before the Spanish *entrada* in the sixteenth century, potters fired with the most commonly available fuels: wood and sometimes coal. Then the settlers came, bringing their livestock, and their livestock began eating the grass and leaving reminders of their presence. It didn't take long for potters to learn that dried animal dung burned quite nicely and was much easier to find, carry, and prepare than coal or dry wood. The animals on these pages have clearly earned their place in this book. In fact, they're truly part of it.

The Indians of the Southwest have been an agrarian society for the last two thousand years, so they took easily and quickly to the raising and tending of the animals the Spanish brought. Now Pueblos and Navajos alike tend all the standard livestock and portray them all affectionately.

One piece in the picture to the right deserves special mention. In a book like this, the natural assumption is that few of the pieces have ever really been used, since they were clearly created as souvenirs. Susanna Manygoats's piggy bank (#4) has a true utilitarian history and saw heavy service. When we bought it, it had a hole the size of a silver dollar punched out of its stomach, created by the seller's daughter (an eight-year-old, if we remember correctly) in a moment of desperate need.

RIGHT: *1) Mata Ortiz, Hector Ortega, 1995; 2) Laguna, M. Kanteena, 1995; 3) Cochiti, ca. 1880; 4) Navajo, Susanna Manygoats, 1990; 5) Laguna, Evelyn Cheromiah, 1993; 6) Mata Ortiz, Marta Gonzalez R., 1997; 7) Navajo, 1995; 8) Navajo, 1995; 9) Navajo, 1995; 10) Navajo, possibly Elsie Benally, 1995; 11) Navajo, Askie Bitsui, 1990; 12) Navajo, possibly Elsie Benally, 1995; 13) Jicarilla Apache, ca. 1980; 14) Navajo, 1995; 15) Navajo, 1995; 16) Acoma, Evelyn Garcia, 1989; 17) Santa Clara, Margaret Gutierrez, 1994; 18) Santa Clara, Dorothy and Paul Gutierrez, 1992; 19) Santa Clara, Margaret Gutierrez, 1994; 20) Navajo, possibly Elsie Benally, 1995. The blue truck is 11¼″ long; the blackware rams' heads on this page are 3½″ snout to snout.*

Poultry

The Spanish probably brought the chickens, but the ducks, geese, and turkeys, we already had. The wonderful prehistoric Ramos Polychrome duck from Paquime in Chihuahua (#14) may have lost his topknot and the handle that went from his neck to his tail, but he hasn't lost one bit of his exuberance. For hundreds of years, Southwestern potters have entertained us with good-natured bird effigies and figurines.

A high percentage of those birds inhabit the farmyard. In fact, some potters have specialized in them. Hopi's Edith Nash made a career out of chicken bowls and baskets in the mid-twentieth century, as #6 and #10 attest. Santa Clara and Hopi potters made bird ashtrays by the dozen, and you can see a few on page 27.

Now, potters give us literal representations of the local poultry as well as representations so abstract that you have to look twice to recognize them as birds. Since the 1940s at Tesuque, they've made them in tan clay and decorated them in poster paint. Twenty-five years before that at Isleta, they put coin slots in their backs. At Santo Domingo in the 1970s, they made bowls out of them. They make them in all sizes at Acoma, they make them in blackware at Mata Ortiz, the Navajos make them in brownware, and at Zuni, Darryl Westika made one that's so strange it defies description.

Today, they've also brought back the prehistoric forms. The parrotlike creation (#17) by Marvis Aragon, Sr., bought at the 1996 Indian Market, is pure contemporary Acoma, but it's an accurate evocation of Anasazi effigy canteens made a thousand years ago.

RIGHT: *1) Mata Ortiz, Jaime Quezada, 1992; 2) Navajo, Betty Manygoats, 1995; 3) Zuni, Travis Penketawa, 1997; 4) Hopi, Evelyn Posthero, ca. 1985; 5) Santo Domingo, Santana Melchor, 1972; 6) Hopi, Edith Nash, ca. 1960; 7) Santa Clara, Jo Ann, 1978; 8) Zuni, Darrell Westika, 1993; 9) Santa Clara, Hemlock, 1993; 10) Hopi, Edith Nash, ca. 1960; 11) Acoma, ca. 1950; 12) Isleta, ca. 1920; 13) Acoma, Sharon Lewis, 1990; 14) Chihuahua, Ramos Polychrome, ca. 1450; 15) Tesuque, ca. 1955; 16) Acoma, ca. 1985; 17) Acoma, Marvis Aragon, Sr., 1995; 18) Hopi, Cheryl Naha, 1992; 19) Tesuque, Terry Tapia, 1983. Betty Manygoats' bizarre Navajo brownware duck jar (#2) is 9½″ high.*

Owls

At Zuni, they defined the form. But not everybody follows the definition. In 1879, an ethnologist named James Stevenson went on a vast artifact-gathering tour for the Smithsonian, and his findings in the 1880–1881 annual report of the Bureau of Ethnology gave us the first full, illustrated overview of Southwestern Indian pottery ever compiled and published. The report leaned heavily in Zuni's direction, and it shows owls that look like they could have been made by the modern potters who made the Zuni pieces in the picture to the right.

Nobody knows how long they've made owls like these at Zuni, but Zuni hardly has an exclusive on owl figurines. In fact, almost everyone else makes them except the Navajos, who associate them with death. (We once heard a Zuni potter offer a good-natured intertribal needle on the subject. He said that Zunis love to put owls in their windows because "they keep Navajos away.")

Most Acoma potters stay close to the Zuni form, despite Stella Shutiva's experimentation with the corrugated body of prehistoric utilitarian pottery, like pitcher #2 on page 14. The farther away you get from Zuni, the more varied the owls become. Here, the northern pueblos of Santa Clara and Pojoaque have given us squatty little figures. At Jemez, Laura Gachupin gives us one of her trademark owls, unlike any other owl that ever existed anywhere else. Moving south to Maricopa, in the Phoenix basin, the owls become simplified effigy jars. And by the time we get down to Mata Ortiz in Chihuahua, the owl comes to us as a hooded effigy just like the prehistoric examples on page 39.

RIGHT: 1) Jemez, Laura Gachupin, 1993; 2) Zuni, ca. 1940; 3) Acoma, Sarah Garcia, ca. 1960; 4) Cochiti, Joseph Suina, 1992; 5) Tesuque, Ka'Ween, 1994; 6) Acoma, Stella Shutiva, 1980; 7) Acoma, ca. 1965; 8) Cochiti, Snowflake Flower, 1997; 9) Acoma, Judy Ortiz, 1992; 10) Zuni, C. Kalestewa, 1992; 11) Zuni, Nellie Bica, ca. 1960; 12) Zuni, Donna Allapowa, 1992; 13) Mata Ortiz, Juan Quezada, Jr., 1997; 14) Zuni, Nellie Bica, ca. 1960; 15) Santa Clara, Margaret and Luther Gutierrez, ca. 1980; 16) Zuni, Rita Edakie, 1992; 17) Acoma, J. Antonio, ca. 1980; 18) Santa Clara, Dorothy and Paul Gutierrez, 1992; 19) Maricopa, Phyllis Cerna, 1990; 20) Pojoaque, Cordelia Gomez, 1994. Stella Shutiva's potbellied owl (#6) stands 5¼˝ high, and Laura Gachupin's prickly bowling ball (#1) is 4˝ in diameter.

49

Frogs & Turtles

The people of the Southwest may take water seriously, but they've always had fun with the water's occupants. Back on page 28, we discussed the Zuni prayer meal basket and the tadpoles, dragonflies, and occasional frogs that adorn it. These water symbols mean a lot to people whose prosperity has depended on good rainfall for a couple of millennia.

If you're given to conventional linear thinking, it follows that they should therefore represent these creatures with a great deal of caution in their arts, fearing that the gods who control these matters might otherwise be offended. Fortunately for those of us who'd rather smile than worry, the Indians of the Southwest don't seem to let things like that bother them. For a thousand years, their frogs and turtles have been almost entirely friendly and no more noble than their mass-culture counterparts in the Saturday morning cartoons.

The turtles seem rather placid, as befits their slow-moving nature, but they're alert, inquisitive, and affable. Whether they're from Hopi, Acoma, San Ildefonso, Zuni or Santa Clara or the Navajo, they all seem like they'd get along just fine. Priscilla Peynetsa's #2 may have a touch of lordliness about the eyes, but none do much to inspire worship, much less strike fear into the heart of the beholder.

If the turtles are benign, the frogs are manic. No tribe of the Southwest needs water more than the Maricopa, yet Mabel Sunn's frog #9 has one of the jolliest, goofiest smiles you'll ever see. Rose Brown's and Martha Arquero's Cochiti frogs (#4 and #11) defy analysis, and even the Mojaves, who credit the frog with stealing fire from the gods and bringing it to the people, couldn't stay serious. They gave us frogs like Annie Fields's #3. When Annie Fields portrayed their hero frog of legend, the firebrand became a cigar—see the one by her son Elmer Gates on the table of contents page.

ABOVE AND RIGHT: *1) Anasazi, Mesa Verde Black-on-white, ca. 950; 2) Zuni, Priscilla Peynetsa, 1993; 3) Mojave, Annie Fields, ca. 1970; 4) Cochiti, Martha Arquero, 1992; 5) Navajo, Rosita Jean, 1995; 6) Cochiti, Rose Brown, 1994; 7) Tohono O'Odham, NA, ca. 1990; 8) Maricopa, ca. 1900; 9) Maricopa, Mabel Sunn, ca. 1950; 10) Hopi, Robert Homer, 1993; 11) Cochiti, Rose Brown, 1994; 12) Zuni, Anderson and Avelia Peynetsa, 1992; 13) San Ildefonso, Wan Povi (Kathy Sanchez), 1994; 14) Maricopa, Phyllis Cerna, 1990; 15) Santa Clara, Dorothy and Paul Gutierrez, 1993; 16) Santa Clara, Anita Suazo, 1994; 17) Acoma, Mary Histia, ca. 1920; 18) Zuni, Gloria Chavez, 1996; 19) Zuni, Agnes Peynetsa, 1995; 20) Santa Clara, Diane Halsey, 1992; 21) Santa Clara, Margaret Gutierrez, 1996; 22) Santa Clara, Anita Suazo, 1997; 23) Santa Clara, Margaret Gutierrez, 1996; 24) San Juan, Lawrence Dili, 1993; 25) Acoma, Caroline Concho, 1993. Martha Arquero's big-mouthed frog (#4) is 6" wide, and the Anasazi cup on this page stands 4" high.*

2
3
4
5
6
7
8
9
10
11
12
13
14
15
16
17
18
19
20
21
22
23
24
25

Creepy Crawlies

No matter how nasty the creature, the portrayals stay affectionate.
The potters of the Southwest bond with nature in all its forms, up to and
including lizards, snakes, and bugs.

The inset on this page shows a quartet of dancing lizards, as jubilant as
ever a group of lizards can be. They cavort atop a squatty jar by Zuni's Noreen
Simplicio, and they exemplify the way the Indian pottery of the Southwest
finds joy in the smallest, least-glamorous pockets of life. As you can see in the
picture to the right, Hopi potters gave us spiders and flies; Cochiti, Zuni,
Jemez, and Maricopa potters gave us lizards; and Acoma, Cochiti, Maricopa,
and Isleta potters gave us snakes.

Even the fearsome rattlesnake appears over and over, especially in
Maricopa pottery. Living as they do in the arid deserts near Phoenix, they
know more than they wish they did about poisonous snakes and, we're told,
decline to make snake pots in the summer because it brings bad luck—you
might step on one. Yet they coexist with the rattlesnake in a surprisingly non-
judgmental way. On a visit to the Hoo-Hoogam Ki Museum in Scottsdale,
owned by and devoted to the Pima and Maricopa and their arts and culture,
we were charmed by a Pima legend on the origin of the rattlesnake. The story
tells of a nice little fellow who went to the meeting of the animals and found
that none of them paid him any attention. He left sadly, and coyote, an ever-
present mischief-maker in Southwestern mythology, took pity on him,
outfitting him by tying a gourd to his tail and placing a devil's claw (a spiky
desert thistle) in his mouth. His instructions were that he should rattle the
gourd to gain attention when he returned to the gathering, and when he
opened his mouth to speak, to show the devil's claw.

They all stopped, looked, and listened, and have ever since.

RIGHT: 1) Zuni, Noreen Simplicio, 1993; 2) Maricopa, ca. 1925; 3) Jemez, Glenda Loretto, 1992;
4) Maricopa, Barbara Johnson, ca. 1980; 5) Zuni, Anderson and Avelia Peynetsa, 1992;
6) Maricopa, G. Stevens, ca. 1970; 7) Maricopa, ca. 1920; 8) Cochiti, Damacia Cordero, ca.
1980; 9) Acoma, Diane Lewis, 1993; 10) Hopi, Art Cody, 1972; 11) Hopi, Sylvia Naha, 1994;
12) Cochiti, ca. 1950; 13) Acoma, Lucy Lewis, 1961; 14) Zuni, Agnes Peynetsa, 1992;
15) Acoma, Rebecca Lucario, 1993; 16) Acoma, Vincent Hansen, 1981;
17) Isleta, Nanette Teller, 1997; 18) Zuni, Tammy Bellson, 1997;
19) Cochiti, Martha and April Arquero, 1995. Damacia Cordero's
lizard (#8) is 11½″ snout to tail; Noreen Simplicio's lizards
stick only an inch above the top of the jar.

1

Waterworld

There's no water shortage in the Southwestern potter's fantasy life. If you'd given us a list of the collections in this book when we first started learning about pottery, and if you'd asked us to name the one that couldn't possibly exist, it would have been this one.

Because rivers are small, seldom flow year-round, and are few and far between; because lakes are miles apart and often dry from year to year; and because the ocean is as foreign to the Southwest as the desert is to most other parts of the country, Southwestern Indians don't have great bodies of water as part of their daily lives.

Yet amazing water creatures exist in Southwestern mythology. The avanyu, the water serpent, wraps around countless pieces from Santa Clara and San Ildefonso like the ones in the inset picture on this page, and it's usually presented quite seriously. Every so often, however, even the avanyu lightens up. It finds two marvelous incarnations in the picture on the right. Isleta's Deborah Jojola created the giant creature that towers over this watery world, while, on a much more intimate scale, Acoma's Mary Lowden tamed the beast and sent the whole family—which includes a dog named "Beer Can"—out for a joyride on the serpent's back (#13).

Zuni and Mata Ortiz have given us fish for our ocean. Cochiti has given us a sea creature, three mermaids, and a bathing beauty. To help us navigate, Maricopa and Jemez have given us canoes. And, as a final, disarming touch, master potter Lucy Lewis, whose large white ollas decorated in excruciatingly accurate fineline detail defined the highest end of modern Acoma pottery, gave us the two silliest little black tadpoles we've ever seen.

There may be little water in the Southwest, but without question, there's a waterworld.

ABOVE AND RIGHT: *1) Santa Clara, ca. 1950; 2) Santa Clara, Minnie Vigil, ca. 1970; 3) Isleta, Deborah Jojola, 1982; 4) Cochiti, Seferina Ortiz, 1995; 5) Cochiti, Seferina Ortiz, 1996; 6) Cochiti, Marie Lowala, 1990; 7) Mata Ortiz, Larige Corona, 1995; 8) Jemez, ca. 1975; 9) Cochiti, Ivan Lewis, 1992; 10) Maricopa, ca. 1935; 11) Zuni, Chris Nastario, 1992; 12) Maricopa, ca. 1925; 13) Acoma, Mary Lowden, 1990; 14) Cochiti, ca. 1960; 15) Acoma, Lucy Lewis (pair), 1961. Deborah Jojola's towering water serpent is 13″ high.*

✳ OTHER STUFF
Tiny Things

Miniatures have been around since prehistoric times. But what you see here is a current phenomenon. Back on page 30, we showed you a thousand-year old, 2¼″-long, Mogollon moccasin-shaped bird effigy/water sipper. These days, the experts call any piece of Southwesten pottery under three inches a "miniature," so that clearly qualifies.

However, there's miniature and there's *really* miniature. A few years back, the potters of the Southwest started trying to outminiature each other, and the competition escalated in the 1990s. A handful of potters have created a whole new category that, for want of a better name, we call "subminiatures." By our definition, it includes pieces an inch or less in their largest dimension.

Some of these pieces come from potters known for larger pieces, like Seferina Ortiz of Cochiti. But to our eye, five specialists stand out. The people who design Silicon Valley's microchips might appreciate some of the accomplishments achieved by Thomas Natseway of Laguna, Judy Shields of Acoma, Geri Naranjo of Santa Clara, Noreen Simplicio of Zuni, Pam Hauer of Taos, and Theresa Wildflower. (Theresa is Chemehuevi, a tribe not shown on the map in the front of the book. It's a small southeastern California tribe with no particular pottery tradition, and she works in the Acoma/Laguna style.)

We thought we'd seen the ultimate in miniaturization when we found Judy Shields' ⅜″-long pig back in 1993, and we treated it as a the be-all and end-all of Southwestern pottery microtechnology in our first book. Then, at the 1996 Indian market, we met Judy and bought our pig's girlfriend, replete with coquettish eyelashes and two-thirds the size of the big guy. They're now happily married, and we're sure that any day now, we'll encounter Judy again, and she'll introduce us to some of their even tinier offspring.

RIGHT: *1) Enlargement of Thomas Natseway's #19; 2) Santa Clara, Geri Naranjo, 1993; 3) Acoma, Santana Titla, 1994; 4) Acoma, Judy Shields, 1994; 5) Santa Clara, Gregory Lonewolf, 1994; 6) Santa Clara, Dolores Curran, 1993; 7) Chemehuevi, Theresa Wildflower, 1995; 8) Zuni, Noreen Simplicio, 1995; 9) Santa Clara, Dorothy and Paul Gutierrez, 1990; 10) Acoma, Judy Shields, 1992; 11) Santa Clara, Dorothy and Paul Gutierrez, 1990; 12) Laguna, Thomas Natseway, 1994; 13) Cochiti, Seferina Ortiz, 1993; 14) Taos, Pam Lujan Hauer, 1993; 15) Laguna, Thomas Natseway, 1994; 16) Acoma or Jemez, ca. 1980; 17) Laguna, Thomas Natseway, 1994; 18) Acoma, Judy Shields, 1996; 19) Laguna, Thomas Natseway, 1995; 20) Acoma, Judy Shields, 1993; 21) Chemehuevi, Theresa Wildflower, 1994; 22) Acoma, Judy Shields, 1996. The giant piece in the group, Geri Naranjo's black and sienna bowl, is 1¼″ in diameter. Mrs. Pig is ¼″ long and ¼″ high.*

57

Poster Paint & Beyond

Back in hard times, tradition took a beating. And store-bought paints gave pottery a new look. The story of the decline and fall of pottery tradition has been told with clucking disapproval in many books. The fingers usually point at Tesuque, the nearest pueblo to Santa Fe and therefore the most accessible to the greedy traders who cared only about profiting from the tourist dollar.

As the chronicles relate, Tesuque potters first learned that you could make more rain gods if you didn't fire them, but just left them in the sun to dry. Then they found that you didn't need to use traditional, hard-to-make earth paints, you could just color them with ink. Then, in the 1920s, they found poster paints, probably down at the Woolworth's in Santa Fe.

Finally, they found that little bowls and jars were a whole lot quicker to make than rain gods. The new era of Depression-spawned tourist pottery had begun. In the 1930s, pots from Tesuque and Jemez like the smaller ones on the opposite page probably sold for a nickel or less, and pottery purists groaned about it for decades. (Some of these have been protected with spray or varnish, others are in their natural, water-soluble state.)

After World War II, potters discovered the new acrylic paints, and still later, the airbrush. By the 1970s, the Navajos and their imitators were producing pieces like the big green thing on the opposite page, and the manufacture of kitsch tourist pottery decorated in commercial paints continues unabated—not always by Southwestern potters. Indian pottery factories from the Dakotas to Florida have been churning out nontraditional pieces for years, and will undoubtedly continue to do so for years to come. The piece inset to the right shows the current state of the art.

RIGHT: *1) Navajo, Warren, 1996; 2) Jemez, CC, 1995; 3) Jemez, 1934; 4) Jemez, ca. 1965; 5) Tesuque, ca. 1940; 6) Navajo, Suti, 1972; 7) Jemez, CC, 1995; 8) Jemez, RL, 1995; 9) Tesuque, ca. 1950; 10) Tesuque, ca. 1935; 11) Jemez, ca. 1940; 12) Tesuque, ca. 1960; 13) Jemez, AL, 1995; 14) Tesuque, Reyes Herrera, 1992; 15) Tesuque, ca. 1960; 16) Tesuque, Reyes Herrera, 1992. The elaborate early Jemez jar (#3) is 7¼″ high, the piece on this page is 6½″ high.*

59

Unborn Collections

The previous pages show 25 collections. Give us a few more years, and we could probably accumulate 25 more. For starters, here are half a dozen other equally obtainable categories. The pocket vases at the bottom of this page hang on the wall to hold anything from ceremonial cornmeal to toothpicks. Square and triangular tiles have been a Hopi tourist specialty for more than a hundred years, meant to serve as trivets for hot dishes. Later potters occasionally put a display stand on the back as on #10.

For most of this century, potters have made architectural models in pottery form. The red domed piece from Santo Domingo is a miniature *horno*, a replica of the pueblo outdoor bread oven, and a starter piece for yet another collection. (There's one from Zia on page 6.) Pottery jewelry shows up from time to time, and there will always be refrigerator magnets. Priscilla Peynetsa's #17 probably started life as a Christmas ornament. And for one more collection, several pieces in this book were made as coin banks.

Finally, there are the hopelessly politically incorrect "whirling logs." The design points in either direction and appears all over the world as a good luck symbol. It used to show up in the Southwest on pottery, rugs, jewelry, and almost everything else. After 1940, however, it only meant one thing: the swastika emblem of Hitler's Nazi Germany. It disappeared from Southwestern art, and collectors have been fascinated by it ever since.

It seems the fascination of Southwestern pottery never ends. It's always imaginative and always highly skilled, but unlike other major art forms, it's seldom self-important or pretentious. Potters speak of their craft with joy and reverence for the clay, and it shows in their work. With the pottery of the Southwest, the art may be serious, but the artists smile.

1

2

3

RIGHT: **Pocket Vases:** *1) Santo Domingo, Thomas Tenorio, ca. 1985; 2) Hopi, ca. 1925; 3) Hopi, ca. 1965.* **Architecture:** *4) Taos, Jevi, 1990; 5) Santo Domingo, Mary Edna and Robert Tenorio, 1994; 6) Santo Domingo, ca. 1975.* **Whirling Logs:** *7) Isleta, ca. 1920; 8) Isleta, ca. 1925; 9) San Ildefonso, ca. 1880.* **Tiles:** *10) Picuris, Anthony Durand, 1996; 11) Hopi, Gwen Setalla, 1994; 12) Hopi, Darlene Vigil, 1990; 13) Hopi, Sadie Adams, 1970.* **Jewelry:** *14) Santo Domingo, Angel Coriz, 1992; 15) Hopi, Lawrence Namoki, 1993.* **Refrigerator Magnets:** *16) Zia, Julia Saiz, 1997; 17) Zuni, Priscilla Peynetsa, 1993. Jevi's church at Taos is 6¼" wide, and the red Hopi pocket vase (#2) stands 4¾" high.*

☀ Index of Pueblos & Potters

The following places and potters appear in the collections on these pages.

*San Felipe,
L. L. Lucero., 1978*

The Authors

ALLAN HAYES   JOHN BLOM

John and Al have been friends since the eighth grade, were college roommates, and were coworkers on the Stanford humor magazine. Al and Carol Hayes started collecting Southwestern pottery seriously in 1992 and infected John and Brenda Blom shortly after. Their joint collection got out of hand so rapidly that they realized they either had to quit or write a book to justify the habit. They decided on the book, and *Southwestern Pottery: Anasazi to Zuni* (Northland Publishing) appeared in 1996. The book gave them their excuse, but it didn't cure them of collecting. It also didn't succeed in making them forget why they started collecting in the first place. Collecting is fun and the art itself is fun. That's why they wrote *this* book.

AL HAYES is chairman and creative director of Hayes Orlie Cundall Inc., a full-service advertising agency located in Sausalito, California.

JOHN BLOM spent most of his working life as vice chairman of Overseas Shipping Company and is currently a director of Robin's Nest Pre-Schools.